IRELAND

IRELAND

THE EMERALD ISLE

MARTIN J. DOUGHERTY

amber
BOOKS

Copyright © 2018 Amber Books Ltd

All rights reserved. No part of this publication may be reproduced,
stored in a retrieval system, or transmitted in any form or by any
means, electronic, mechanical, photocopying, recording, or otherwise,
without prior written permission of the copyright holder.

Published by
Amber Books Ltd
United House
North Road
London
N7 9DP
United Kingdom
www.amberbooks.co.uk
Instagram: amberbooksltd
Facebook: amberbooks
Twitter: @amberbooks

Project Editor: Sarah Uttridge
Designer: Jerry Williams
Picture Research: Terry Forshaw, Justin Willsdon

ISBN: 978-1-78274-662-1

Printed in China

4 6 8 10 9 7 5

Contents

Introduction 6

Beaches and Coastlines 8

Forts, Castles and Country Houses 62

Hills and Mountains 104

Religious Places 150

Towns and Cities 180

Picture Credits 224

Introduction

When the glaciers retreated after the last Ice Age, rising sea levels separated what is now Ireland from mainland Britain. Lying on the western fringe of Europe, this new large island was heavily influenced by the Atlantic Ocean, creating a climate characterized by mild winters and heavy rainfall, with occasional severe storms blowing in from the sea.

Ireland has been inhabited by humans for at least the last 12,000 years. By the time the Roman Empire arose in

Europe, Ireland was populated by Celtic people, whose Gaelic language is still spoken today and whose art and music live on in modern society. Ireland was never conquered by the Romans, and survived incursions by Norsemen from Scandinavia and later Normans from England. It was not unchanged, though; society evolved with each new set of outside influences. The Celtic-Christian Church flourished in Ireland from the 5th century, with traditional Celtic motifs counterpointing the formality of the mainstream Church. Today's Ireland is part of European society, yet retains a character all its own.

ABOVE:
Ha'penny Bridge in Dublin
OPPOSITE:
Cobh Cathedral

Beaches and Coastlines

Ireland stands on the fringes of Europe, surrounded by seas. Its western coasts face the Atlantic Ocean, with the milder Irish Sea to the east and the Celtic Sea to the south. The latter are linked by St George's Channel, while the North Channel separates the Irish Sea from the Atlantic coasts of Scotland.

It is not possible to be far from the sea anywhere in Ireland, but its coasts vary considerably in character. Some areas are sandy and sufficiently reminiscent of northern France that they have been used in war movies to represent Normandy. Others are rock-strewn, with forbidding cliffs in places. This has much to do with the underlying rock structure of Ireland and the prevailing weather conditions. The rock that underlies Ireland was once part of two different continents, brought together by drifting plates. The northwestern part of Ireland is geologically similar to the North American plate, while the southeastern part is European in character.

In places there are very old volcanic rocks close to the surface, with softer limestone in other areas. The erosion of these rocks, along with sediment deposits and the action of glaciers in the Ice Age, contributed to the varied character of Ireland's coastline. Many of its beaches have been awarded Blue Flag status, indicating that they comply with stringent requirements for quality of bathing water and proper beach management.

OPPOSITE:
Achill Island, County Mayo
Lying off the west coast of Ireland, Achill is its largest island. It has some of the highest sea cliffs in Europe and has been inhabited for around 5,000 years. Today it is connected to the mainland by the Michael Davitt Bridge.

**Black Castle,
County Wicklow**
Taking advantage of a
naturally strong position on
a high promontory, the Black
Castle at Wicklow was built in
the 1100s to protect the nearby
coast from invasion. Its date
of construction is unclear, but
is known to be before 1174.

OPPOSITE:
Tory Island, County Donegal

The currach is a traditional boat design, with a wooden frame over which fabric is stretched. In the past this would have been animal hides; today, canvas is typically used. This boat lies on the shore at Tory Island.

BELOW:
Tory Island, County Donegal

Many legends surround Tory (Toraigh) Island, located off the coast of County Donegal. The supernatural Fomorians were said to have their stronghold there. At the end of the Big Key, a rocky promontory, lies An Tor Mor; 'the big tower'.

OPPOSITE:

Keem Beach, Achill Island, County Mayo
The white sands of Keem Beach lie on the south side of Croaghaun Mountain, the highest and most westerly of Achill Island's mountains. The northern face of the mountain includes some of the highest sea cliffs in Europe.

BELOW:

Doolin, County Clare
Sunset over Doonagore Castle near Doolin in County Clare on the west coast of Ireland, built on the site of an earlier fortification. A nearby cave holds the Great Stalactite, which at 7.3m (24ft) is claimed to be the longest in the Northern Hemisphere.

RIGHT:

Brittas Bay, County Wicklow
Once associated with smuggling, Brittas Bay is today a popular recreation spot for the people of Dublin. Lifeguard stations have been installed at many beaches, but many of them are only manned for part of the year. This is not least because some beaches are less than inviting in the depths of winter.

LEFT:

Shipwreck on the Irish coast
The combination of a rugged coastline and often harsh Atlantic weather means that shipwrecks are not uncommon on the Irish coast. Some were a consequence of war, from Spanish galleons to the super-dreadnought HMS *Audacious*. Most, however, fell victim to the common perils of the sea.

RIGHT:

Corrib River, County Galway
The Corrib River is short but deep, and is popular with white-water kayakers. It flows from Lough Corrib into Galway Bay at the town of Galway on the west coast of Ireland, 6km (4 miles) away.

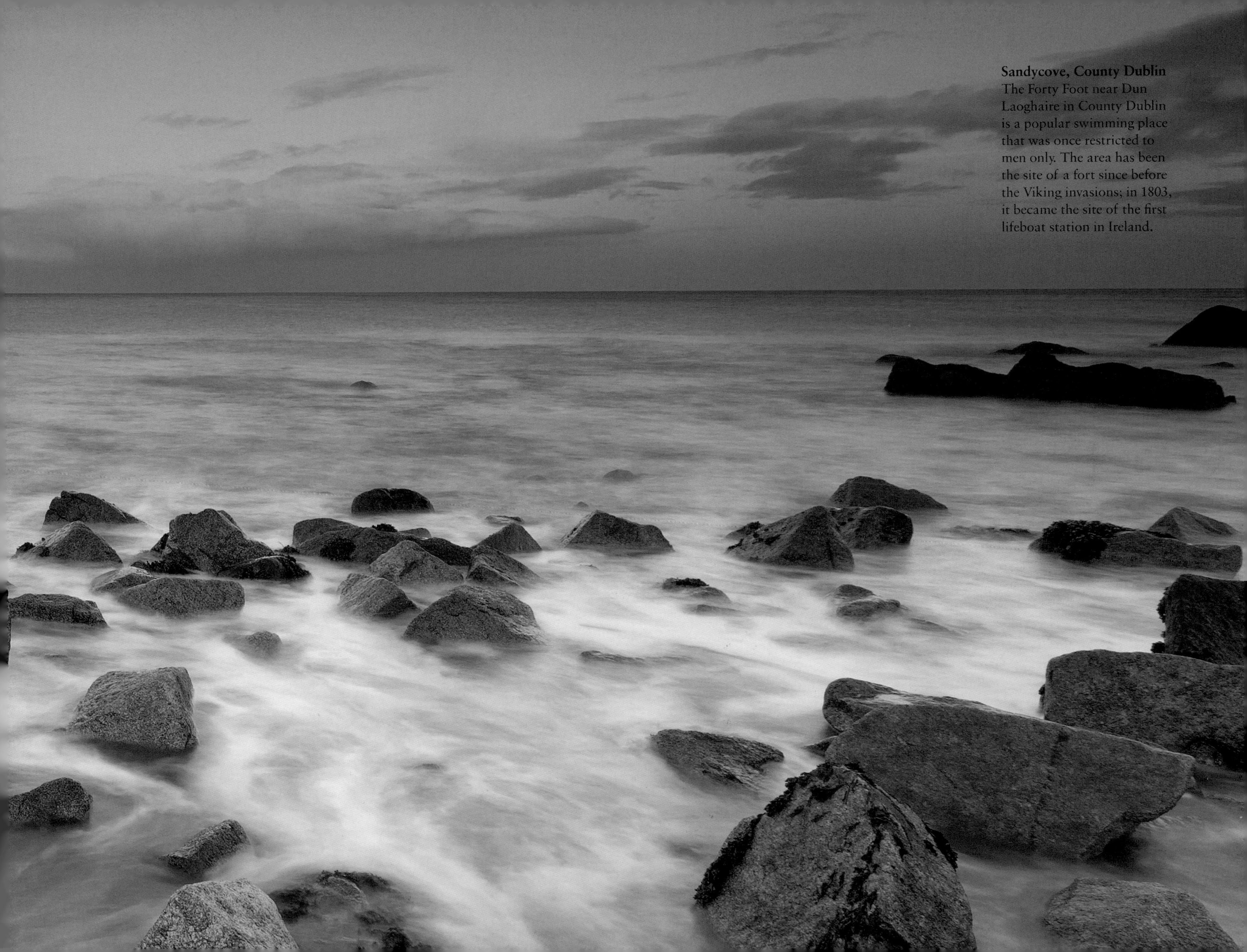

Sandycove, County Dublin
The Forty Foot near Dun Laoghaire in County Dublin is a popular swimming place that was once restricted to men only. The area has been the site of a fort since before the Viking invasions; in 1803, it became the site of the first lifeboat station in Ireland.

OPPOSITE:

Rush, County Dublin
The region around Rush in
County Dublin has been
inhabited since the Stone Age
and may have been a Roman
outpost in Ireland. In the 18th
century it became associated
with smuggling, though since
then it has become a popular
holiday destination.

RIGHT:

Ballybunion, County Kerry
Lying on the west coast of
Ireland, Ballybunion has a
number of tidal caves along
its rocky shore. It is a popular
location for surfing, with
two beaches known as the
men's beach and the ladies'
beach after their traditional
segregation by cliffs.

LEFT:

Giant's Causeway, County Antrim

The Giant's Causeway on the north coast of County Antrim is composed of basalt columns – most of them hexagonal – formed when lava cooled around 60 million years ago. Similar formations exist on the Scottish coast, originating from the same lava plain.

RIGHT:

Giant's Causeway, County Antrim

There are around 40,000 columns making up the Giant's Causeway, some as much as 10–12m (32–39ft) high. The area is a UNESCO World Heritage Site, and is considered to be one of the natural wonders of the British Isles.

ABOVE:
Baltimore, County Cork
The navigation beacon at Baltimore lies on the southern coast of County Cork. It was built in the late 1840s to replace an earlier structure that had fallen into disrepair. It is known locally as 'Lot's Wife' after the Bible story of a woman turned into a pillar of salt.

OPPOSITE:
Fanad Lighthouse, County Donegal
Standing close to Lough Swilly, one of the few glacial fjords in Ireland, Fanad Lighthouse was built after the loss of HMS *Saldanha* in 1812. The ship was carrying a large quantity of gold bars, not all of which have been recovered. 300 lives were lost.

Coastal County Sligo
The Wild Atlantic Way runs
through County Sligo on
its way from the Inishowen
Peninsula in the north to
County Cork in the south.
The coast here is a mix of
lowlands and mountains,
with many islands just off
the coast.

LEFT:

Kinvara, County Galway

Galway Bay is one of the most important waterways in Ireland. It is noted for the Galway Hooker, a small sailing craft designed to deal with the local sea conditions. This example lies on the beach near Kinvara, once a busy port exporting locally gathered seaweed.

LEFT BELOW:

Cobh, County Cork

For a time known as Queenstown, Cobh in County Cork has long been an important port for both local and international shipping. Emigrants took ships to the New World there, and RMS *Titanic* set sail from Cobh. Many of the small piers built to support local boats are now in disrepair.

RIGHT:

Rossbeigh Beach, County Kerry

The schooner Sunbeam was driven ashore on Rossbeigh Strand over a century ago. After being just visible above the water since 1903, the remains were washed up on Rossbeigh Beach by a severe storm in 2014. Long preserved by the sea, the wreck quickly began to deteriorate.

**Cliffs of Moher,
County Clare**
Over 200m (656ft) high at their
highest point, the Cliffs of
Moher are a popular tourist
destination and are home to
many species of birds. The site
was fortified in ancient times,
and more recently was used
as a lookout point during the
Napoleonic Wars.

LEFT:

Coastline, County Donegal
Although some of the beaches in County Donegal are close to major population centres and thus popular tourist destinations, much of the region's coast is all but deserted. Numerous islands lie off the coast, most of them small and uninhabited.

RIGHT:

Ballintoy, County Antrim
The small fishing port of Ballintoy near Ballycastle declined over the years until there were less than 200 inhabitants. It featured in the fantasy TV drama *Game of Thrones* as a pseudo-medieval port town. The wild scenery of other parts of Ireland has featured in other television and film productions, including recent *Star Wars* films.

**Mulranny Bay,
County Mayo**
Taking its name from the
Gaelic name for 'hill of
the ferns', Mulranny is famous
for its plant life. The region
is also connected with Grace
O'Malley, an infamous 'pirate
queen' who supported Irish
insurrections against English
rule in the 16th century.

County Mayo
Many rural areas of County
Mayo are very sparsely
populated, with a sense of
peaceful timelessness that
makes them popular with
walkers and nature-lovers.

**Clogher Head,
County Louth**
The fishing village of
Clogherhead is named for
the nearby Clogher Head and
has the distinction of having
the only beach-launched
lifeboat in Ireland. It lies on
the shore of the Irish Sea,
between Dundalk Bay and
the Boyne estuary.

LEFT:

Blackrock diving boards, Salthill
The Blackrock diving boards at Salthill in Galway are popular with outdoor swimmers. An annual Christmas Day event sees large numbers of people jumping into the sea to raise money for charity, and many local school-leavers take a dive to symbolize their new status.

RIGHT:

Mussenden Temple, County Londonderry
Constructed as a library in 1795, Mussenden Temple was built in the pseudo-Classical style popular at the time. Its position atop the cliffs near Castlerock was threatened until work was undertaken to prevent further erosion of the cliffs.

Downpatrick Head, County Mayo
The spectacular 40-m (131-ft) stack at Downpatrick Head near Ballycastle is said to have been formed when St Patrick separated it from the mainland, marooning a local chieftain who refused to convert to Christianity.

LEFT:
Dundalk, County Louth
The port of Dundalk lies on
Dundalk Bay, an inlet of the
Irish Sea. Most of the bay is
shallow, and is surrounded by
tidal flats and salt marshes.
The region's maritime history
has produced more than a
few shipwrecks.

OPPOSITE:
Roundstone, Galway
The village of Roundstone
is renowned as a haven for
artists. The surrounding
countryside has a great
variety of plant life and
wild flowers. Dominated by
Errisbeg Mountain, it bears
the marks of glaciers from
the last Ice Age.

LEFT:
**Valentia Island,
County Kerry**
Warmed by the Gulf Stream,
Valentia Island has a mild
climate suitable for lush
vegetation. Standing stones
and fossilized tracks of
prehistoric creatures are
counterpointed by a modern
weather-monitoring station.

RIGHT:
**Fanore Beach,
County Clare**
The area around Fanore
Beach, on the west coast of
Ireland in County Clare, has
been inhabited by humans
since the Stone Age. The
region was a centre for the
creation of stone tools around
7000-8000 BC, with later tombs
and structures indicating
continued habitation.

**Killary Fjord,
County Galway**
There is much academic debate
about whether Killary Fjord
is in fact a fjord – some say
it is the only one in Ireland
– or a fjard, or exactly what
designation should apply. A
fjard differs from a fjord in that
it is wide and not surrounded
by steep cliffs, but is otherwise
formed in much the same way.

LEFT:
**Malin Head,
County Donegal**
County Donegal boasts
the most northerly point in
mainland Ireland, at Malin
Head on the Inishowen
Peninsula. Its shore is of
international scientific interest
due to changes caused when
the land 'sprang up' after the
ice sheets melted.

OPPOSITE:
**Ballynacregga,
County Galway**
The tiny village of
Ballynacregga lies on the
shore of Lough Corrib,
the largest lake in the Irish
Republic. Its name translates
as 'town of the rock'.

OPPOSITE:

The Wormhole, Aran Islands

The Wormhole (Poll na bPéist) is named for a sea-dwelling serpent of mythology. Water enters the natural rectangular pool through an underwater cave, spraying upward in time with the waves even though there is no visible connection to the sea.

RIGHT:

Carrick-a-Rede rope bridge, County Antrim

The current rope bridge at Carrick-a-Rede is a modern creation, but there has been a similar – at times rather precarious – bridge in place for the past three or four centuries. Originally used by salmon fishermen, the bridge today carries tourists wishing to visit the island.

LEFT:
Dunquin Pier, County Kerry
This road leads to Dunquin,
the most westerly settlement
in Ireland. Out to sea lie
the Blasket Islands, now
uninhabited but once home to
a rich cultural tradition. This
apparently placid stretch of
water saw several ships of the
1588 Spanish Armada wrecked.

OPPOSITE:
**Great Blasket Island,
County Kerry**
The Blasket Islands were
evacuated in 1953, at the
request of the inhabitants
who were regularly cut off
from the mainland. Unable
to provide even life-saving
services at times, the Irish
government resettled the
population, leaving the shells
of their cottages to decay on
the abandoned islands.

Malin Beg, County Donegal
Silver Strand Beach at Malin Beg on the western tip of County Donegal is a popular location for divers, due to the clarity of local waters. The area attracts other outdoor sportspeople, notably climbers and hang-gliding enthusiasts.

LEFT:
**Portmagee,
County Kerry**
Portmagee is located south
of Valentia Island in County
Kerry. The nearby Skellig
Islands – visible out to sea –
were once home to an early
Christian monastery, which is
well preserved largely due to
its inaccessibility. The islands
were used as a location in
recent *Star Wars* films. They
are also a bird sanctuary.

RIGHT:
**Dingle Peninsula,
County Kerry**
This image shows Sybil Point
in Ballyferriter Bay on the
Dingle Peninsula. The peaks
known as the Three Sisters
form part of the spine of the
peninsula, lying to the north
of Ballyferriter itself.

LEFT:
Dingle Peninsula, County Kerry
Dingle, located on the peninsula of the same name, was constructed by the Norman invaders, and grew to become an important route for goods in and out of Ireland. Today it is mainly a fishing port.

BELOW:
Dingle Peninsula, County Kerry
The port at Dingle has had a long association with Spain, and has played host to fishing fleets from elsewhere in the British Isles. Inshore boats from the Isle of Man have berthed there, along with trawlers from Lowestoft.

OPPOSITE:
Dingle Peninsula, County Kerry
The western tip of the Dingle Peninsula is the westernmost part of mainland Ireland. Beyond it lie the Blasket Islands, which were inhabited until the 1950s. Today, they are visited by ferries bringing tourists from the mainland.

OPPOSITE:

False Bay, County Galway

The plentiful seafood available along the western coast of Ireland made the Connemara region of Galway an attractive location for early humans to settle. Evidence has been found of middens dating back to the Mesolithic era or perhaps earlier.

BELOW:

Tramore Beach, County Donegal

There are several areas of coast named 'Tramore' in Ireland, as it translates from Gaelic as 'big beach'. This particular big beach is in County Donegal near Rossbeg, in an area that has been inhabited since prehistoric times.

Forts, Castles and Country Houses

Ireland has a long history of fortification, from earth and timber forts to complex stone castles. Some were built to protect against invaders, some to protect the invaders from the people they thought they had conquered. Others were intended to defend territory against rivals from nearby.

The simplest fortifications were usually built on a hill or promontory, with ditches dug to make access difficult and the earth from them piled into steep-sided ramparts. These were often topped with wooden palisades, which in some cases could be removed when not needed. Earthwork forts of this type made use of naturally occurring defensive terrain, sometimes cutting off one end of a steep ridge or an area close to clifftops. This reduced the number of defensive works required, allowing concentric ditches to be constructed for the same amount of effort as an encircling ditch on lower ground. Stone walls were sometimes used to create a hill or cliff fort in this manner, or the defences might incorporate nearby boulders.

By the middle ages, stone castles had become the norm. The science of castle-building advanced right through the medieval era, and even after gunpowder artillery had made the castle obsolete there were those who continued to build them. Many castles of this period were converted into manor houses, or renovated in a fanciful pseudo-medieval style.

Later fortifications also exist, especially on the coasts. Lookout towers and artillery forts intended to protect against invasion in the Napoleonic era were sometimes used as military barracks long after the threats they were built to counter had passed.

OPPOSITE:
Blarney Castle, County Cork
Built in the mid-1400s on the site of an earlier fortification, Blarney Castle has survived siege and passed through several owners' hands. The famous Stone of Eloquence (the Blarney Stone) is incorporated into the walls.

Ross Castle, Killarney

Like many fortifications of the late 1400s, Ross Castle takes the form of a central tower house surrounded by a bawn. Originally referring to any defensible cattle enclosure, the word 'bawn' came to mean a fortified area enclosed by a curtain wall with reinforcing towers.

RIGHT:
Camden Fort Meagher

Once gunpowder artillery became common, a vertical wall was simply too vulnerable to cannon fire and the art of fortification had to evolve. Built in the 1860s to defend Cork harbour and originally named Fort Camden, Fort Meagher is well dug in, with underground passages like this one.

Markree Castle, County Sligo
Built in the 1400s to protect crossings of the River Unshin, Markree Castle was remodelled in the 19th century with an emphasis on comfort rather than defence. Today it is a country hotel.

Adare Manor, County Limerick

Originally built in the 17th century, Adare Manor in County Limerick was rebuilt in the 19th century in its present form. A fortified manor house had existed on the site much earlier, perhaps dating from the 13th century.

RIGHT ABOVE:

Birr Castle, County Offaly

Like many fortresses, Birr Castle was converted over time to make it more comfortable to live in. During the 19th century it was partially rebuilt and given a cosmetic overhaul, with Gothic features added as was fashionable at the time.

RIGHT BELOW:

Birr Castle, County Offaly

The gardens at Birr Castle today include an adventure playground and a three-storey treehouse. Platforms in the trees are linked by rope bridges and scramble nets. The castle is also famous for having what was once the largest telescope in the world.

OPPOSITE:

Duckett's Grove House, County Carlow
Originally a Georgian manor, Duckett's Grove House was redesigned in the early 1800s to incorporate pseudo-Gothic features. The battlements were never intended for defence – such features had been obsolete for centuries – but were a popular decoration for stately homes in the period.

BELOW:

Duckett's Grove House, County Carlow
The grand house at Duckett's Grove fell into disrepair early in the 20th century after the heiress to the estate was left a single 'angry shilling' from a very large estate. The estate was eventually bought by Carlow County Council and made into a park.

Castle Roche, County Louth
According to legend, during the 1230s the wealthy Norman widow Rohesia de Verdun offered to marry (and thereby make very rich) the man who built her a suitable castle. She kept her word, but threw her new husband out of a window on their wedding night.

LEFT:

**Redwood Castle,
County Tipperary**

Built in typical tower house style by the Normans around 1200, Redwood Castle was subsequently expanded and altered before falling into ruin in the 1600s. It was renovated as a private residence in the 1970s.

RIGHT:

**Dunluce Castle,
County Antrim**

Built in the 1500s on the site of an earlier structure, the defences of Dunluce Castle were later augmented with cannon from a wrecked Spanish galleon. Part of the castle fell into the sea in the 1800s, though according to legend this happened much earlier.

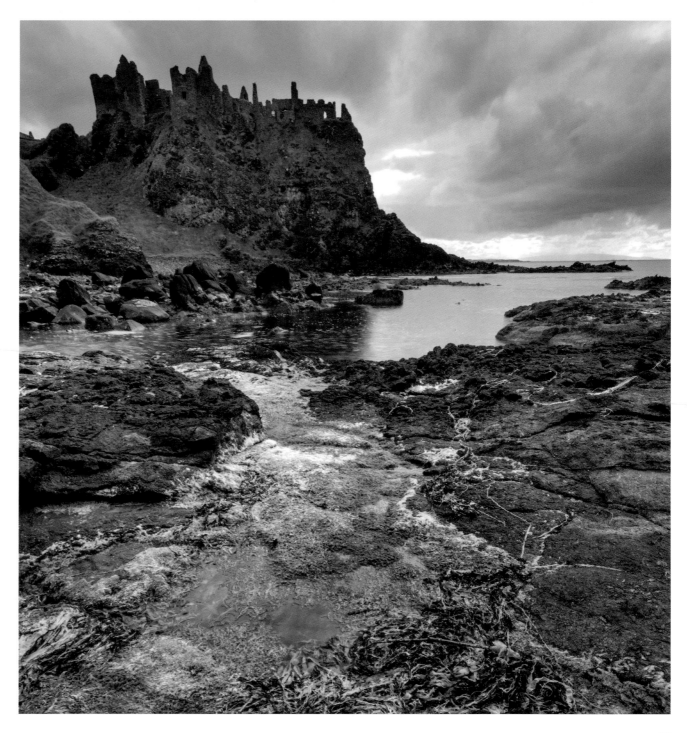

**Dunamase Castle,
County Laois**

The Rock of Dunamase has been the site of a fortification since the 800s, though perhaps not continuously. The current stone castle was built in the late 1100s. Its current ruined state is largely the result of slighting (making a castle useless, usually by blowing part of it up) by Cromwell's forces in the 1650s.

LEFT:

**Bunratty Castle,
County Clare**
Bunratty Castle is actually
the fourth to stand on the site.
Earlier fortifications have been
replaced or destroyed over the
centuries. The original castle
at Bunratty dated from 1250
or so, though there may have
been a Norse settlement on
the same site even earlier.

OPPOSITE:

**Ballybunion Castle,
County Kerry**
It is not surprising that the
site of Ballybunion Castle in
County Kerry was previously
the site of a promontory
fort, cutting off a defensible
area with the cliffs providing
added security. The present
castle remains date from
around 1500.

Ardmore, County Waterford
Although constructed in
a Gothic style, this watch
tower at Ardmore was built
around 1800. At that time
the most likely threat was an
invasion from France, which
was building an empire that
spanned Europe.

LEFT:

**Leamaneh Castle,
County Clare**

Located on the fringe of the
Burren, a region of karst
landscape in County Clare
that is the smallest of Ireland's
six national parks, Leamaneh
Castle was originally built
as a large five-storey tower
house. It was later altered
and extended to make it
more habitable but fell into
disrepair in the late 1700s.

RIGHT:

**Grace O'Malley's Tower,
Achill Island**

The tower at Kildavnet was
probably built around 1429
by the O'Malley clan. It is
more commonly associated
with the legendary Grace
O'Malley, or Granuaile, who
was born a century later; the
structure is generally known
as Grace O'Malley's Tower.

OPPOSITE:
Powerscourt Estate, County Wicklow
By the 1730s, when Powerscourt Estate was converted from
a castle to a manor house, defence was less important than
ostentation. The approaches to a house were carefully laid out
to create the maximum possible impact upon a visitor.

ABOVE:
Trim Castle, County Meath
Constructed to defend a crossing point on the River Boyne,
Trim Castle was built in the late 1100s. It was later owned by
Richard of York and, later still, by Sir Arthur Wellesley, Duke
of Wellington.

LEFT ABOVE:
Castletownsend Castle, County Cork
By the 1600s, traditional castles were obsolete but still fashionable. Many owners chose to build in a style reminiscent of much earlier times, creating confusion for modern observers with a mix of decorative and non-functional features.

LEFT:
Crom Castle, County Fermanagh
The Earls of Erne acquired the site of what is now Crom Castle in 1609. The present castle was built in 1820 on the site of the earlier structure. It is a fine example of the Victorian style of building, though construction was completed shortly before Queen Victoria came to the throne.

ABOVE:
Johnstown Castle, County Wexford
The castle at Johnstown was originally constructed in the late 12th century. Later owners remodelled the defensive structure into a more comfortable home, which was given ornamental lakes and gardens in the mid-19th century.

Rock of Cashel, County Tipperary
The Rock of Cashel was traditionally the seat of the kings
of Munster, but was given to the Church in 1101. The earlier
structures were built over, with few traces remaining. The
earliest surviving structure is the round tower, dating from
around 1100.

OPPOSITE:
**Lismore Castle,
County Waterford**
The castle-builder's art is
demonstrated by this bartizan
– an overhanging tower – at
Lismore Castle. Originally
intended to protect the
corner of a wall from attack,
these structures were often
added as a decorative feature
precisely because they were
difficult to build.

RIGHT:
**Donegal Castle,
County Donegal**
The site of Donegal Castle,
on a bend in the Eske River,
was considered strategically
important enough to be
fortified since at least as early
as the Viking invasions of
Ireland. The present castle
was built in 1474 but suffered
severe damage on various
occasions. It was renovated
and altered in the 1600s
before falling into disrepair.

LEFT:

MacDermott's Castle, County Roscommon

MacDermott's Castle is built on one of the many islands in Lough Key, which is said to have formed when a powerful druid named Cé was buried there. Cé was wounded in battle against the supernatural Fomorians, who were defeated and driven from Ireland.

RIGHT ABOVE:

Ballysaggartmore Towers, County Waterford

Built in the early 1800s near Lismore in County Waterford, the Ballysaggartmore towers are follies serving to decorate an estate and impress visitors rather than having any real practical function. Plans to build a manor house in similar style apparently failed for lack of funds.

RIGHT BELOW:

Mallow Castle, County Cork

Although built during the late 1500s as a home rather than a fortress, Mallow Castle – like many contemporary great houses – was constructed with a mind to defence. Its towers and corners allow attackers to be engaged with firearms as they approach.

Castle Desmond, County Cork

Castle Desmond lies on the River Maguire near Adare. Constructed in the 12th century, it was captured by the English during the 'Desmond Rebellion' of 1569–1573 and later slighted by Cromwell's forces in 1657. The castle lay derelict until the 1990s, when restoration began.

ABOVE:

King John's Castle, County Limerick

The site of King John's Castle at Limerick has been fortified since the early 900s. The present castle was built on what is now known as King's Island, beginning in 1200. It survived a siege in 1642, albeit with serious damage, and was renovated starting in 2011.

Dunguaire Castle, County Galway
Lying on Galway Bay near Kinvara, Dunguaire Castle is constructed as a tower house with a surrounding curtain wall, both of which have been the subject of restoration work. It was the seat of the ancient kings of Connaught.

Puxley Manor, County Cork
Puxley Manor was built close to the ruins of Dunboy Castle, which was taken by the English in 1602 and the defenders all executed. The new manor was said to be cursed as a result. It was burned by the IRA in 1921, then partially restored in the 2000s to become a hotel. The project failed for lack of funding.

RIGHT:
Foulksrath Castle, County Kilkenny
Built in the 1400s on the site of an earlier fortification, Foulksrath Castle is a five-storey Anglo-Norman tower house. After falling into disrepair, the castle was renovated in the mid-20th century and was for a time a youth hostel.

Muckross House, County Kerry
Muckross House is located in the Killarney National Park.
It was built in 1839–43, and in the following decade received
ornamental gardens. These were updated in the next century
and still exist today. The estate also has an open-air museum
dedicated to rural life in early 20th Century Ireland.

Ormond Castle, County Tipperary
Built in the 1560s in the new Elizabethan style, Ormond Castle
was unusual for the era in that it was not fortified although it
incorporated some features from an earlier castle on the site.
It was restored in the mid 20th century.

Dublin Castle, Dublin
Built in the 13th century,
Dublin Castle may have
replaced an earlier fortification
on the same site. It was updated
over the centuries, with most
surviving structures dating
from the 1700s. The castle
has been a seat of successive
governments; Irish presidents
are still inaugurated there.

Belfast Castle, Belfast
The present Belfast Castle is the third to stand upon the
site. The first dated from the late 1100s and was replaced
by a new fortification built in 1610. It was destroyed by fire,
and eventually supplanted by the present castle, which was
completed in 1870.

Belfast Castle, Belfast
The external staircase was a later modification, commissioned
in 1894 after the castle passed into the ownership of the Earls
of Shaftsbury, who had provided financial assistance during the
building process.

Hills and Mountains

The terrain of central Ireland is characterized by boggy lowlands for the most part, with higher ground elsewhere. Although an island cannot possess huge mountain chains to rival the Alps or the Rockies, Ireland has its share of mountains. The highest is Carrauntuohill, in the Macgillycuddy's Reeks range in County Kerry. This range contains several of Ireland's tallest mountains. The western coast of Ireland is noted for spectacular sea cliffs, including the highest sea cliffs in Europe. These are located on Achill, the largest of Ireland's many offshore islands.

This landscape owes much to the underlying rock. Ireland was formed in two parts, which drifted together and collided around 440 million years ago. This pushed up some of Ireland's mountains, notably those of Donegal. Conditions changed over time, with what is now Ireland spending millions of years submerged. As a result, the rock of Ireland is very mixed. There are regions of granite and other volcanic rocks in some areas, limestone and chalk in others. The karst landscape of the region known as the Burren has its own unique character.

Elsewhere, the landscape is varied. Some areas show the effects of glaciation during the last Ice Age, with steep valleys carved out before the ice retreated, often leaving freshwater loughs (lakes) fed by the new valley's rivers. Not all loughs are freshwater, however; the word 'lough' is the same as the Scots 'loch' and can indicate a sea inlet, fjord or bay. Many of these sea loughs are steep-sided, with tall cliffs towering above the water.

OPPOSITE:
Wicklow Mountains, County Wicklow
Occupying much of County Wicklow and extending into neighbouring regions, the Wicklow Mountains are largely composed of granite. The region's character owes much to the action of ice in the last Ice Age and is today recognized as a natural conservation area.

LEFT:

Narrow-gauge railway, County Antrim

The Giant's Causeway and Bushmills Railway follows the track bed originally laid for a tram system. It is a steam-powered narrow-gauge railway, giving access to the UNESCO World Heritage Site at the Giant's Causeway in County Antrim.

LEFT BELOW:

Bog Village Museum, County Kerry

Bogs were economically important all over Ireland, with turf and peat cutting essential to the local economy. The bog village in County Kerry is a recreation of traditional life during the 1800s. Some structures are original, having been dismantled and brought to their new location.

RIGHT:

Mourne Mountains, County Down

The Mourne Mountains are a granite range, designated as an area of outstanding natural beauty. It is possible to see the Isle of Man and mountains in England from some peaks. The mountains and their surrounding lowlands are popular with walkers and outdoors enthusiasts.

LEFT:

**Mourne Mountains,
County Down**
'The Mountains of Mourne'
is a popular song written in
the 19th century by Percy
French. It contrasts life in the
big city as experienced by
an Irish émigré with home,
where the mountains sweep
down to the sea. It has been
covered many times, and
quoted in other songs.

RIGHT:

**Mourne Mountains,
County Down**
The tallest peak in Northern
Ireland is Slieve Donard, in
the Mourne Mountains. Part
of the mountain and those
nearby are now owned by the
National Trust, but proposals
to give the region National
Park status have been
complicated by the amount
of private land that lies within
the proposed park.

The Burren, County Clare
The Burren region gets its name from the anglicization of Boireann, or Great Rock. It is a karst landscape formed by the action of water on soluble rock such as limestone and gypsum, with a layer of soil added in the south by the action of glaciers.

LEFT:

Glencar Waterfall, County Leitrim

Lying just north of Glencar Lough, Glencar Waterfall was immortalized in the poem *The Stolen Child* by William Butler Yeats. Other waterfalls nearby include the much higher but somehow less romantic Devil's Chimney.

OPPOSITE:

Wicklow Mountains, County Wicklow

Located south of Dublin, Wicklow Mountain National Park covers much of the uplands in County Wicklow. In addition to protecting the flora and creatures of the region, the park provides educational activities including guided walks that highlight the region's diverse wildlife.

**Wicklow Mountains,
County Wicklow**
The highlands of Ireland
are home to many ruined
structures; the legacy of farms
that fell on hard times or
became victims of conflict.
Many are close to roads or
visitors' centres and can be
explored at leisure. Others are
very remote and can only be
glimpsed at a distance.

Croagh Patrick, County Mayo

Croagh Patrick is associated with St Patrick, but may have been
a religious site long before the coming of Christianity.
The chapel at its summit dates from 1905, but there is evidence
of an earlier structure dating from the 5th century.

Derryveagh Mountains, County Donegal

Mount Errigal is the highest peak in Donegal, at 751m (2464ft).
It is flanked by Mackoght, which at 555m (1821ft) is sometimes
called 'Little Errigal'. Both are part of the Derryveagh
Mountains, a region popular with hillwalkers and climbers.

LEFT:

**Glenbarrow Waterfall,
County Laois**

Glenbarrow Waterfall lies in
the Slieve Bloom Mountains,
which are among the oldest in
Europe. Once around 3700m
(12,140ft) high, the mountains
have been eroded over the
eons to not much over 500m
(1640ft). This is still a fair size
for the generally low-lying
interior of Ireland.

LEFT BELOW:

Union Wood, County Sligo

Ireland was once extensively
forested, though much of
this coverage has been lost to
farmland and other human
uses. The ancient deciduous
forests of County Sligo are
popular with walkers and
nature-lovers, with many of
the best walks waymarked.

RIGHT:

**Dark Hedges,
County Antrim**

The beech trees of the Dark
Hedges were planted three
centuries ago to line the
approach to Gracehill House.
This stretch of road is said to
be haunted by the spirit of a
servant at the house, who was
buried in a nearby cemetery.

OPPOSITE:
**Mount Errigal,
County Donegal**
The tallest of County
Donegal's peaks, Errigal is one
of the 'Seven Sisters', known
locally as the Derryveagh
Mountains. Its distinctive
colouration is due to quartzite,
a metamorphic rock formed
from sandstone.

RIGHT:
**Black Valley,
County Kerry**
The Black Valley is on
the Kerry Way, a popular
walking and cycling route
through the county. It lies in
the Macgillycuddy's Reeks
mountain range, which
contains all the mountains
in Ireland that are above
1000m (3280ft).

Tipperary Mountains
County Tipperary is named for its main town, which dates from the 1300s. Much of the county is rural, with several mountain ranges. The area surrounding the River Suir is known as the Golden Vale, and is renowned for dairy farming. The vale stretches beyond the county's borders.

LEFT:

County Louth
Named after the warrior-king god Lugh, County Louth is the smallest in Ireland. It has a long history of conflict, having been fought over by Vikings, Normans and Scots as well as the English. Most famously, it was the site of the Battle of the Boyne in 1690.

OPPOSITE:

Ring of Kerry, County Kerry
The Ring of Kerry is a popular tourist route; the driving equivalent of the Kerry Way. It runs through the countryside of County Kerry past picturesque ruins and wild landscapes as well as through several towns, starting with Killarney.

LEFT:

Skellig Michael Island, County Kerry

The two Skellig Islands, Little Skellig and Skellig Michael, lie off the Iveragh Peninsula in County Kerry. Also known as Great Skellig, Skellig Michael is inaccessible, which may be one reason why it was chosen as the site for a monastery during the early middle ages.

RIGHT ABOVE:

Beehive clocháns on Skellig Michael Island

The clochán is a quintessentially Celtic construction, typically found in southwestern Ireland. It is essentially a beehive-shaped structure of drystone construction, with a corbelled roof.

RIGHT BELOW:

Skellig Michael Island, County Kerry

Scenes from *Star Wars: The Force Awakens* were filmed on Skerrig Michael island. Not only was the scenery perfect, but there is also a resonance between Luke Skywalker's desire for isolation and that of the real-world medieval monks.

OPPOSITE:

St Fiachra's Garden, County Kildare

The Irish National Stud's Japanese garden contains an area dedicated to St Fiachra, patron saint of gardens. It includes a replica of a monk's hermitage and a statue of the saint himself in addition to its natural features.

RIGHT:

Bogland in County Offaly

County Offaly is largely made up of boglands, whose turf and peat traditionally provided the inhabitants with fuel for cooking and building materials. The bogs also preserved whatever fell into them, including these 5000-year-old trees.

LEFT:

Lough Corrib, County Galway

A little less than half the size of Lough Neagh in Northern Ireland, Lough Corrib is the largest body of water in the Republic of Ireland. In the 1100s the first canal in Ireland was cut, linking Lough Corrib to Galway Bay.

BELOW:

Lough Corrib, County Galway

Lying on the Atlantic coast, Galway receives its share of Atlantic storms but the climate is also moderated by the ocean. Winters can at times be very cold, but on the whole Galway has an agreeable climate.

OPPOSITE:

Killarney National Park, County Kerry

The three Lakes of Killarney – Muckross Lake, Lough Leane and Upper Lake (seen here) are a popular feature of the Killarney National Park. Upper Lake is the smallest of the three, which are surrounded by the Macgillycuddy's Reeks mountain range.

OPPOSITE:

Dun Eochla, County Galway

The stone ringfort of Dun Eochla stands on Inishmore, largest of the Aran Islands in Galway Bay. The fort was built around 550–800 AD, of drystone construction. The Aran Islands have several similar fortifications, some of which are known to date from as early as 1000 BC.

ABOVE:

Clifden, County Galway

The town of Clifden is widely considered to be the informal capital of Connemara, a cultural region in County Galway. The existing fishing village was expanded by the D'Arcy family, whose estate was nearby, in the early 19th century to become an important local port.

OPPOSITE:
Rural landscape, County Kerry

Killarney National Park in County Kerry has the only red deer population in mainland Ireland, and retains the largest concentration of native forest remaining. Since 1981, the park has been a UNESCO Biosphere Reserve, and is the subject of several conservation projects.

RIGHT:
Torc Waterfall, Killarney National Park

Close to Muckross Lake, the deepest in Ireland, Torc Waterfall lies at the base of Torc Mountain. 'Torc' in this case refers to the Irish word for a boar; according to legend, the hero Fionn mac Cumhail slew a magical boar on the mountainside.

OPPOSITE:

Derryclare Lough, County Galway
Located just south of the Twelve Bens mountain range, Derryclare Lough is a freshwater lake well known for its fishing. The nearby area is famous for transatlantic firsts; the town of Clifden was the site of the European end of Marconi's wireless telegraph, and in 1919 Alcock and Brown's Atlantic crossing ended in a nearby bog.

BELOW:

Benbulben Mountain, County Sligo
In Irish legend, hero Fionn mac Cumhail sought vengeance on the warrior Diarmuid who had run off with his intended wife, Grainne. Fionn mac Cumhail tricked Diarmuid into fighting an enchanted boar at Benbulben Mountain, where he was killed.

**Top of Benbulben
Mountain, County Sligo**
The height of Benbulben
Mountain creates a unique
environment where plants
carried to the region by
glaciers in the last Ice Age
have survived. The only
known population of fringed
sandwort in Ireland grows
atop the mountain.

LEFT:
Gweedore, County Donegal
Many areas of Ireland are renowned for their retention of the traditional Irish culture and language; Gweedore on the coast of County Donegal, is perhaps the most famous of them. Gaoth Dobhair, to use the traditional Irish name, is a parish rather than a single town or village, and includes extensive areas of open countryside.

OPPOSITE:
Beara Peninsula, Southwest Ireland
Lying partially in County Kerry and partly in County Cork, the Beara Peninsula contains two mountain ranges: the Slieve Miskish and the Caha Mountains. Both are of sandstone and neither is particularly high, with no peaks above 500m (1640ft).

Galtee Mountains, Southern Ireland
The characteristic shape of the Galtee Mountains is due to their height. As the tallest inland mountain range in Ireland, the tops of the Galtees were above the glaciers during the last Ice Age, and thus subject to natural weathering while the lower slopes experienced glacial action.

OPPOSITE:
Slieve League Cliffs, County Donegal
At over 600m (1969ft) high, the Slieve League cliffs are among the highest in Europe. A tower was built there in the early 1800s to warn of possible French invasion. Long before that, the site was a religious centre, probably predating Christianity.

BELOW:
Lough Leane, County Kerry
Largest and most northerly of the Three Lakes of Killarney, Lough Leane lies in the shadow of the Macgillycuddy's Reeks mountain range. There are numerous islands in the lake, and from it the River Laune flows into Dingle Bay.

RIGHT:
Diarmuid and Grainne's Cave, County Sligo
Like many natural shelters, this cave system in County Sligo is associated with the tragic story of Diarmuid and Grainne, who were pursued by Fionn mac Cumhail across Ireland. The caves were formed underwater, but are now located high above sea level.

OPPOSITE:

Belfast Hills, Northern Ireland

Lying close to the capital of Northern Ireland, the Belfast Hills include Divis, Black Mountain and Cavehill. The region is popular with walkers and nature lovers, with spectacular views of the surrounding loughs and mountains.

RIGHT:

Blue Stack Mountains, County Donegal

With their tallest peak at Croaghgorm ('bluestack'), the Blue Stack Mountains divide the southern part of County Donegal from the north. As with many remote areas, the remains of abandoned farm buildings are dotted around the landscape, often far from any other habitation.

LEFT:

Doo Lough, County Mayo
One of a chain of loughs ultimately draining into Killary Harbour, Doo Lough shows the signs of a glacial landscape that also created the fjard at Killary.

OPPOSITE:

Lough Tay, County Wicklow
The Cloghoge Valley contains Lough Tay and Lough Dan. Much of the surrounding land is private, but the Wicklow Way runs nearby and access is possible to Lough Dan by way of the Wicklow National Park.

Religious Places

Before Christianity reached Ireland, Celtic beliefs were widespread. With its tales of heroes, monsters and supernatural beings, this vibrant religion continued to exert a powerful influence over the culture of Ireland's people long after conversion took place. Indeed, the conversion of Ireland to Christianity was something of a two-way street.

St Patrick is normally credited with bringing Christianity to Ireland, arriving around 432 in defiance of Church laws that did not permit a bishop (as Patrick was at the time) to leave his post. He wandered around Ireland preaching to anyone who would listen, persuaded rulers to build churches and appointed clergymen to run them. Irish Christianity took on a distinctly Celtic flavour, and while missionaries from Ireland were enthusiastic about spreading the word, it was not quite the same as the stuffy mainstream Christianity coming out of Rome. Celtic Christianity was a little more vibrant, and incorporated many pagan designs in its art. Some of the traditional folk-tales took on a Christian slant, with bishops and saints featuring in the place of otherworldly heroes.

Irish missionaries spread Christianity to England, Scotland and beyond; even to Iceland. When the first Norsemen arrived there they found a community of Irish monks, who wisely left soon afterward. The Norsemen also came to Ireland, adding their own influences to the developing religious landscape of Ireland. Today's Ireland is predominantly Christian – though with fairly major differences of opinion about how to go about it – but does not recognize any one religion above others and guarantees freedom of worship to all faiths.

OPPOSITE:
Quin Abbey, County Clare
Built in the early 1400s on the ruins of a castle that occupied the site of an earlier monastery, Quin Abbey belonged to the Franciscan order. It was largely destroyed in 1650 by Oliver Cromwell's forces and only partially repaired.

LEFT:

St Gobbans Church, County Antrim

The tiny non-denominational church at Portbraddan was the smallest in Ireland from its construction in the 1950s until its demolition in 2017. There is some debate as to whether it was a 'proper' church, but it was a popular venue for weddings and other religious events.

OPPOSITE:

Ennis, County Clare

The county town of County Clare, Ennis has been a major religious centre since at least 1240, when the king of Munster, Donnchadh O'Brien, gave instructions for a large church to be built. It was later taken over by the Franciscan order, but suffered in the Dissolution of the Monasteries in the 16th century,

**Dunlewey Church,
County Donegal**
At the foot of Mount Errigal
in County Donegal lies the
Poisoned Glen, said to be the
resting place of the poisonous
eye of the Fomorian
Balor. Dunlewey Church,
consecrated in the 1850s,
overlooks the glen. In recent
years it has been the subject
of restoration work.

LEFT:

**Poulnabrone portal tomb,
County Clare**

The dolmen, or portal tomb,
at Poulnabrone dates from
the Neolithic period, around
3600 BC. Excavation at the site
found evidence of over twenty
burials, some adult and some
children, along with tools
and pottery.

OPPOSITE:

**Clonmacnoise,
County Offaly**

The monastery at
Clonmacnoise was founded
by St Ciarán in the 540s. In its
long history it became a centre
for learning and a burial place
for the High Kings of Ireland.
It had fallen into disrepair
by the 1550s when it was
destroyed by English troops.

Kylemore Abbey, County Galway
Kylemore Castle was built by Mitchell Henry in 1867 as a gift for his wife. Along with the castle, Henry built a Victorian walled garden and many walkways throughout the 13,000 acre estate. In 1920, the Irish Benedictine Nuns purchased the castle and lands and it was converted into an Abbey.

Bective Abbey, County Meath
Founded in 1147, Bective Abbey expanded and rebuilt over the centuries before being confiscated from its Cistercian owners in the Dissolution of the Monasteries. The church dates from the 13th century; the cloisters from almost two centuries later.

**Galway Cathedral,
Galway City**
Begun in 1958 and completed
in 1965, Galway Cathedral is
the most recently built stone
cathedral in Europe. It stands
on the banks of the Corrib
River on a site previously
occupied by the city jail.

LEFT:

**Glendalough,
County Wicklow**

According to legend, the
Celtic cross was invented by
St Patrick, who combined the
Christian cross with a circle
representing either the sun or
the moon, both worshipped
by pagans, either to try to win
them over or to demonstrate
the supremacy of his Church
over their traditional faiths.

RIGHT:

**Glendalough,
County Wicklow**

Formed by glacial action and
fed by the River Poulanass,
Glendalough means 'valley
of the two lakes'. There was
originally one lake, separated
by a delta built up from
sediment brought by the river.
The Poulanass Waterfall,
upstream from the lakes, is
popular with walkers.

LEFT:
Glendalough,
County Wicklow
The monastery at Glendalough was founded in the 6th century by St Kevin and flourished until 1398 when it was destroyed in a raid. During this time, the church was gradually expanded and additional buildings were added. Some of these survive, including the 30m (98ft) tall round tower.

BELOW:
Caldragh Cemetery,
County Fermanagh
Although it is called a Janus figure, this stone in Caldragh Cemetery on Boa Island represents a Celtic deity rather than the Roman Janus. The term is applied loosely to refer to the fact that it has two faces.

RIGHT:
Skellig Michael,
County Kerry
Skellig Michael was home to a community of no more than a dozen or so monks during its period of habitation. One reason its clocháns and standing stones are so well preserved is the inaccessibility of the island.

Kilcatherine Cemetery, County Cork
Standing on Coulagh Bay, Kilcatherine's ruined church dates
from the 7th century. It is named for St Caithighearn, who
was instrumental in bringing Christianity to the region. St
Caithighearn is sometimes referred to as the 'cat goddess'
for reasons that remain unclear.

Newgrange megalithic passage tomb, County Meath
Consisting of a mound entered by a passage with internal
chambers opening off it, the tomb at Newgrange dates from
around 3200 BC; during the Neolithic era. An opening in the
roof allows sunlight to illuminate the interior at sunrise on the
winter solstice.

OPPOSITE:
Claregalway Abbey, County Galway
The Franciscan abbey at Claregalway was founded around 1250 but fell victim to conflict in the mid-1500s. For a time it was used as a barracks by English troops and was not treated kindly. Although the monks eventually returned, they were unable to repair the damage and neglect the buildings had suffered.

BELOW:
Ballybunion, County Kerry
For the past century or so, the Ballybunion area has been known for its golf courses. The region has been inhabited for much longer than that, however, with an ancient tradition of sacrifices to the Celtic god Manannan and more recent Christian churches.

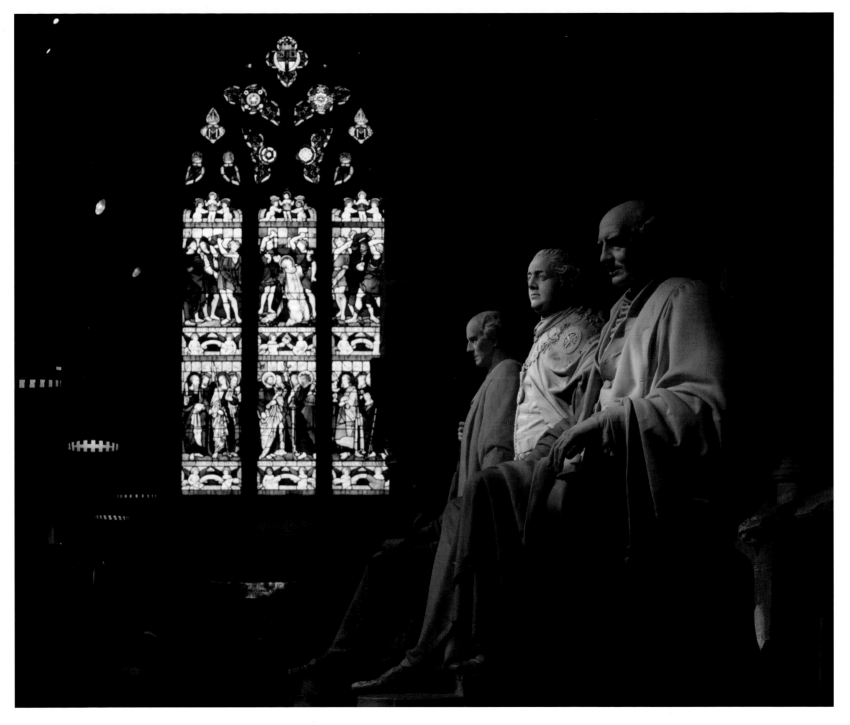

OPPOSITE:

St Patrick's Cathedral, Dublin

Dublin is distinctly unusual in that it has two cathedrals. Christ Church Cathedral is the seat of the Archbishop of Dublin, while St Patrick's is the national cathedral for the entire nation. It was founded in 1191, and remains in use for national ceremonies as well as local worship.

RIGHT:

St Patrick's Cathedral, Dublin

There are over 200 monuments of various sorts in St Patrick's Cathedral. Some are simple plaques, some elaborate stained glass and some are statues. The oldest is a stone effigy of the first Archbishop of Dublin, Fulk de Saundford, and dates from the late 1200s. Many of the statues commemorate religious figures, writers and academics.

LEFT:

**Boyle Abbey,
County Roscommon**
Founded in 1161, Boyle Abbey
was part of a project to bring
European monks to Ireland
in the hope of making its
Church fall into line with
the mainstream Catholic
faith. It was built on a classic
Cistercian plan, with work
finished around 1220.

LEFT BELOW:

**Boyle Abbey,
County Roscommon**
Like most religious buildings
of its time, Boyle Abbey
was decorated with carved
representations of kings,
saints and the occasional
gruesome gargoyle. These
were probably created by
local craftsmen, though they
were subject to European and
English influences.

RIGHT:

**Celtic crosses,
County Sligo**
The exact meaning of the
Celtic cross is open to
some debate. Some believe
it represents a triumph of
Christianity over paganism;
some a melding of the two.
There are many who take it
in a more general context to
represent a land of ancient
traditions and supernatural
mysteries.

OPPOSITE:

Inishmurray Island, County Sligo

The island of Inishmurray was inhabited by a few dozen people until the late 1940s, when the population moved to the mainland. The island was once home to a monastery, founded in the 6th century, which is known to have been the subject of Viking raids.

BELOW:

Slane Abbey, County Meath

The town of Slane is known to have been inhabited since the Neolithic era. According to legend, St Patrick lit a fire celebrating Easter at Slane, in view of the High King's seat at Tara and in defiance of an edict that only the ceremonial fire there was permitted at the time.

LEFT:
Muckross Abbey, Killarney
Founded in 1448, the Franciscan abbey at Muckross had a troubled history. It was founded on the site of a much earlier monastery, probably dating from the 6th century. Muckross Abbey was raided at various times and later attacked by Oliver Cromwell's forces, who drove the monks away.

BELOW:
Drombeg Stone Circle, County Cork
The stone circle at Drombeg probably dates from the Bronze Age, 1500–500 BC. There are signs that nearby habitation spanned a very long period. The circle consists of seventeen stones, one of which is an 'altar' stone aligned to receive sunlight at the winter solstice.

OPPOSITE:
Gougane Barra, County Cork
Founded as a monastic site by St Finbarr in the 6th century, Gougane Barra is still a destination for pilgrimages and a popular place for weddings. The present oratory was built in the 1900s.

OPPOSITE:

**Rosserk Abbey,
County Mayo**

Little is known about the
history of Rosserk Abbey.
A church was known to exist
upon the site in 1198, but
there is no indication when
it was built. The abbey itself
is inferred from historical
documents to have been in
operation by 1441, but again
no direct records exist.

RIGHT:

**Ballintoy Church,
County Antrim**

The church at Ballintoy
was built in the early 1800s,
replacing a previous structure
thought to date from the
early 1600s. The earliest
known record of this church
dates from 1635, though it is
possible that an even earlier
church may have existed upon
the same site.

Towns and Cities

At the end of the last Ice Age, Ireland was connected to mainland Britain and to Europe by land bridges. As the ice sheets retreated and the land warmed, humans began to migrate into the newly available territory. It is not entirely clear when the first humans entered what is now Ireland; in all likelihood, small groups wandered in from time to time, initially leaving few traces.

The land bridges were eventually inundated by rising sea levels, and for the next few thousand years these people migrated according to the availability of food; hunting in the forests or combing the beaches for shellfish. Farming became prevalent around 6500 BC, with the rise of bronze-working following around 2500 BC. Farming communities were generally small, but there was a gradual drift into towns and eventually cities. Many of Ireland's major settlements can trace their origins back to an ancient market town, metalworking centre or port, often with a history of continuous habitation. Settlements built by Norse and later Anglo-Norman invaders also survived into the modern era, becoming part of Irish society in a process that was not without conflict.

Some of these towns were fought over repeatedly. Some gained walls and castles, some cathedrals and grand government buildings. Later came railway stations and industrial centres. Yet the pattern of modern streets might be oddly familiar to someone who lived in the same spot 2000 years ago; the continual evolution of Ireland's towns ensured that many of the original settlement patterns remain.

OPPOSITE:
Queen's University of Belfast, Belfast
Founded as Queen's College Belfast in the 1840s, Queen's University of Belfast can trace its origins back to the beginning of that century. The main campus is centred on the Lanyon Building, seen here, with associated colleges elsewhere in the city.

LEFT:
Limerick City, County Limerick
Lying on the River Shannon, the city of Limerick is one of the largest in Ireland. King's Island, where the central part of the city is located, is known to have been inhabited since the 800s and may have had a settlement long before.

RIGHT ABOVE:
Bishop Gate, Londonderry
Bishop Gate was one of the four original city gates of Londonderry, along with Butcher Gate, Ferryquay Gate and Shipquay Gate. It has two stone heads, one facing in and one outward, representing the rivers Boyne and Foyle respectively.

RIGHT BELOW:
Crane Street, Dublin
Dublin is an old city, officially founded in 988 but probably dating from an earlier era. Vestiges of its long history remain in the form of old buildings, cobbled streets and the occasional horse-drawn conveyance.

Sandymount Station, Dublin
The development of railways had huge economic and social impact, permitting a degree of mobility that had not previously existed. Many modern rail lines follow the path of original tracks laid down in the early age of steam.

Belfast, Northern Ireland
Inhabited since the Bronze Age, the city of Belfast grew up as a port on the River Lagan. It expanded rapidly into a major city in the 17th and 18th centuries, largely as a result of a huge linen manufacturing industry exporting goods through the port.

LEFT:

**Galway Dock,
County Galway**
Like many coastal cities, Galway developed as a seaport, supporting large fleets of fishing vessels such as the Galway Hooker. Today, the port handles large commercial ships as well as cruise liners and a host of smaller craft.

OPPOSITE:

Bachelors Walk, Dublin
Dublin lies on the lower reaches of the River Liffey, which rises in the Wicklow Mountains. Bachelors Walk is a quayside street that, according to legend, was a popular promenade for the city's bachelors. The reality is more prosaic; it was named after a property developer.

LEFT:

Waterford Walls, Waterford
The Waterford Walls project is a large-scale art exhibit making use of the city's walls, including derelict sites that would otherwise be an eyesore. During the creation of the art pieces there is also a cultural festival involving music, educational workshops and food.

RIGHT:

The Four Courts, Dublin
Standing on the banks of the River Liffey, the Four Courts is named for its original function. It remains an important legal centre, although which courts it has housed has changed over time. The building was badly damaged in civil war early in the 20th century and subsequently rebuilt.

LEFT:

Trinity College, Dublin
Founded in 1592, Trinity College was to be the first of the colleges of the University of Dublin, though ultimately it ended up being the only one. Many of its buildings date from an expansion programme in the 1700s.

RIGHT ABOVE:

The Guildhall, Londonderry
After the destruction by fire of the previous guildhall, dating from the 1700s, Londonderry's new Guildhall was constructed in 1887. It was built in the neo-Gothic style popular at the time, and has recently been renovated to restore its stained glass and stonework.

RIGHT BELOW:

Sligo, County Sligo
The Fleadh Cheoil na hEireann is the all-Ireland festival of traditional music. Qualifying rounds take place in many locations – in this case, Sligo – with the final taking place at a different location each year. The event includes parades and concerts as well as the competitive stages.

LEFT:
Ha'penny Bridge, Dublin
The first pedestrian bridge across the Liffey, the Ha'penny Bridge was opened in 1816. Its name is derived from the toll charged to cross it, which was the same amount as the river ferries it made obsolete.

LEFT BELOW:
North Earl Street, Dublin
One of the major retail areas of Dublin, North Earl Street is named for Henry Moore, Earl of Drogheda, who was responsible for much of the development in the area. Among its features is a statue of the author James Joyce.

RIGHT:
River Lee, Cork
The city of Cork stands on the River Lee, with the city centre on an island between two channels of the river. Upstream is a hydroelectric power project; downstream lies Cork Harbour, which was probably the site where local urbanization began during the Viking era.

River Foyle seen from Waterside Station, Londonderry

Londonderry Railway Station is generally known as Waterside Station as it stands on the banks of the River Foyle. The fast flow of the Foyle makes the construction of bridges across it a particular problem.

OPPOSITE:

Peace Bridge, Londonderry
Opened in 2011, Peace Bridge is one of three across the River Foyle in Londonderry. It also spans the railway tracks near Waterside Station and is part of a project intended to improve integration between parts of the city with traditionally very different political leanings.

RIGHT:

Lagan Bridge, Belfast
Various plans have been put forward for new bridges across the Lagan over the years, but it was not until 2015 that the new Lagan Weir Pedestrian and Cycle Bridge was opened. The nearby Beacon of Hope statue was constructed in 2007.

LEFT:

Old Fruit Market, Dublin
The Old Fruit Market was opened in 1892 to replace the scattering of small private markets that existed in the area. The city council was concerned about the quality and cleanliness of the goods being sold, the possibility of unfair prices and their inability to ensure that the correct tax was being paid.

OPPOSITE:

St George's Market, Belfast
Constructed in the 1890s, St George's Market is the oldest such market to have been in continual operation. Centralized shopping areas of this kind represented a social change taking place at the time, and in some ways can be likened to modern supermarkets.

LEFT:

Dublin, Ireland

Many buildings in the city of Dublin date from the Georgian period; the 1700s and early 1800s. Hallmarks of the style include traditional brick construction, symmetry and overall neatness as well as very impressive durability. Large areas of these houses have outlasted newer construction.

RIGHT:

O'Connell Street, Dublin

What is now O'Connell Street, named in honour of the 19th-century nationalist Daniel O'Connell, existed in much narrower form in the 1700s. It was widened and renamed from Drogheda Street to Sackville Street, achieving its modern identity in 1924.

OPPOSITE:

Daly's Footbridge, Cork
Named in honour of a local businessman who contributed to the cost of construction, Daly's Bridge is better known to locals as 'shaky bridge' due to its response to rapid movement. It is the only suspension bridge over the River Lee in Cork.

RIGHT:

Samuel Beckett Bridge, Dublin
Reminiscent of a harp, Samuel Beckett Bridge is designed to move, permitting large ships to pass by on the River Liffey. It was opened in 2009 as part of an urban regeneration scheme and named in honour of Nobel Prize-winning writer Samuel Beckett.

LEFT, LEFT BELOW:
Irish pubs
Recent years have seen increasing numbers of people visiting Ireland's cities to sample the beer and enjoy the atmosphere of an Irish bar. A night in the pub has to be pretty special to bring in people from other countries.

OPPOSITE:
Historic Irish pubs
The 'traditional Irish pub' is a social institution that has spread around the world. Some of the pubs in Ireland itself are traditional in the more literal sense – they have not changed in decades or even centuries.

LEFT:

**The English Market,
Cork City**

The English Market in Cork
City was constructed in the
mid-19th century, on the site
of an earlier market dating
back to 1788. The building
is a fine example of the
Victorian architectural style.

OPPOSITE:

**The Old Library,
Trinity College, Dublin**

Founded in 1592, the Old
Library later became a
copyright library, holding
copies of thousands of works
to enable their authors and
publishers to prove copyright.
It is home to the Book of
Kells, a lavishly illustrated
early medieval manuscript.

LEFT:

Titanic Museum, Belfast
Built on the site of the
former Harland and Wolff
shipbuilding yards, the Titanic
Museum tells the story of
the great liners built there,
including the tragic maiden
voyage of the *Titanic* herself.

RIGHT:

Sightseeing Wheel, Belfast
Constructed in 2007, the
sightseeing wheel was always
intended to be a temporary
feature, initially for six
months. It was sufficiently
popular to remain open
for much longer, though it
attracted criticism for its
location close to the
Titanic Memorial.

OPPOSITE:

Temple Bar, Dublin

The Temple Bar pub is one of several located in the Temple Bar area of Dublin. Much of the land in the immediate area was reclaimed from the River Liffey in the 1700s, with what is now Wellington Quay built in the early 1800s.

RIGHT:

Kinsale, County Cork

As a port on the south coast of Ireland, Kinsale was a logical choice for the landing of Spanish troops intending to attack England. After this force was defeated, a fort was built to prevent further landings. Today the town is best known for fishing and its yacht marina.

OPPOSITE:
River Liffey Islandbridge, County Dublin
Salmon fishing is popular on the Liffey as well as many other rivers in Ireland. The Islandbridge for which this area is named was the result of constructing a mill race, which produced an artificial island.

BELOW:
Famine Memorial, Dublin
Statues on Custom House Quay in Dublin commemorate the Great Famine of 1845–49, which resulted from the failure of the potato crop, among other factors. Around a million people died, and many more emigrated in search of work abroad.

213

Queen's University, Belfast
The main building of Queen's University was designed by
Charles Lanyon to impress all who approached, but insufficient
funding was available to complete the rear to the same standard.
Lanyon also designed the university library, undertaking later
extension work as an initially anonymous bid.

Botanic Gardens, Belfast
Located close to Queen's University, the botanic gardens have existed since 1828 but were only fully opened to the public in 1895. Like the nearby university, the gardens were designed by 19th-century architect Charles Lanyon.

ALL IMAGES:
Guinness Brewery, Dublin
Within the St James Gate brewery is the Guinness Storehouse, which was originally a fermentation plant. Today it is a visitor's centre and museum to the history of Guinness-making, while production goes on elsewhere on the site.

The U2 Wall (Windmill Lane Studios), Dublin
Famous as the location where U2 recorded their early work, Windmill Lane Studios operated from 1978 to 1988 before moving to a new venue. The original site was demolished in 2015, though a section of the 'U2 Wall' with its fan graffiti remains.

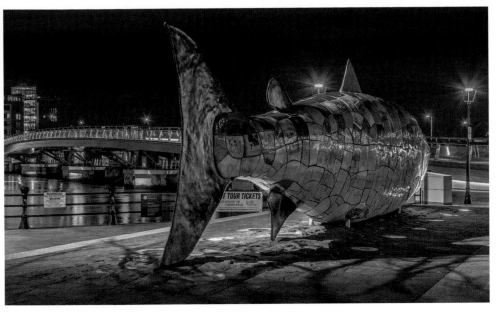

LEFT:

Big Fish Sculpture, Belfast

Also known as the Salmon of Knowledge but inevitably known as The Big Fish, this sculpture stands on the banks of the Lagan in Belfast. Each of its scales contains information about the city and its history.

BELOW:

Graffiti, Location Unknown

Opinions are divided as to whether graffiti of this sort is art or not, but it certainly requires artistic talent to create. Designs are sometimes associated with local culture, sometimes with specific individuals.

LEFT:

Galway Hooker, Galway
The Galway Hooker is a traditional sailing vessel associated with the Galway area. The design shows various overseas influences but has evolved into a form well suited to local conditions, with a sharp bow and a tumblehome hull form widening towards the waterline.

LEFT BELOW:

Poolbeg Lighthouse, Dublin Bay
Constructed in 1768 and later rebuilt, Poolbeg Lighthouse was converted to run on oil in 1786. It is one of three lighthouses in Dublin Bay. The lighthouse stands on the Great South Wall, one of the longest seawalls in Europe.

RIGHT:

Blennerville Windmill, County Kerry
Built in 1800, Blennerville Windmill is the only working wind-powered mill in Ireland. It fell into disrepair in the late 1800s, but was restored towards the end of the 20th century and is now a tourist attraction in addition to its commercial operations.

OSITE:

toria Square Shopping ntre, Belfast

e 35m-diameter (115ft) ss dome of the Victoria uare Shopping Centre is gh enough to permit all- und views of the city. The ntre was opened in 2008 as rt of an urban regeneration ogramme for the area.

GHT:

ublin City Hall

uilt between 1769 and 779, Dublin City Hall was riginally intended to have an pen ceiling. Concerns about he weather led to a revised esign with a dome of stained lass. Restoration work was arried out from 1998 to 2000.

Picture Credits

Alamy: 20 (Rafal Rozalski), 32 (DMc Photography), 48 (Jon Arnold Images/Doug Pearson), 52 (Dennis Frates), 53 (De Luan), 54/55 (Ian Dagnall), 56 (Dennis Frates), 57 (Brian Jannsen), 58 bottom & 59 (Stephen Smith), 61 (Holger Burmeister), 83 (Blickwinkel/RuS Hoffmann), 84 & 86 top (Image Broker/Martin Siepmann), 86 bottom left (Brian Jannsen), 86 bottom right (Travelib Ireland), 87 (Bickwinkel/McPhoto/OPR), 88 (Eye Ubiquitous/Hugh Rooney), 89 (Paul Mayall Ireland), 91 bottom (George Munday), 96 (Design Pics), 99 (David Lyons), 109 (Craige Bevil), 117 (Scenicireland.com/Christopher Hill), 132 (Scenicireland.com/Christopher Hill), 133 (Martin Siepmann), 145 top (AMC), 146 (DMc Photography), 148 (Peter McCabe), 150 (David Lyons), 152 (Clearview), 160/161 (Hemis/Walter), 164 (Ian Dagnall), 165 top (Image Broker/Werner Maling), 166 (John Gollop), 171 (Peter Oshkai), 172 top (David Lyons), 172 bottom (Martin Siepmann), 175 (Steppenwolf), 176 top (Martin Siepmann), 180 (Radharc Images/Joe Fox Liverpool), 187 (Anne-Marie Palmer), 188 (Phil Crean A), 191 bottom (Reallifephotos), 192 bottom (deadlyphoto.com), 196 & 197 (Brian Jannsen), 198 (Paul Mayall Ireland), 199 (Paul Lindsay), 204 bottom ledft (Giannis Papanikos), 204 bottom right (Tim Graham), 208 (Eduardo Blanco), 212 (Design Pics), 213 (Ian G Dagnall), 216 top (Jon Sparks), 218 (Joe Fox Liverpool), 222 (B O'Kane), 223 (Phil Crean A)

Alamy/Gareth McCormack: 58 top, 60, 98, 121, 131, 145 bottom, 149, 165 bottom, 168, 173, 174, 178, 179

Dreamstime: 14 (Slim79), 15 top (Grafxart), 23 (Thomasamm), 28 bottom (Hakbak), 30/31 (Tomasz Skoczen), 43 (Steve Uttley), 45 (Janmiko1), 62 (Michael Walsh), 75 (Jacek Kodaj), 102 & 103 right (Anna & Piotr), 103 left (Navorolphotography), 106 top (Leonid Andronov), 106 bottom (Daniel M Cisilino), 119 (Vander Wolf Images), 130 bottom (Julian Dewert), 140 (Paul Brady), 141 (Steve Allen), 142/143 (Pierre Leclerc), 153 (Pajda83), 157 (Smolnickaquienquiera), 159 (Daniel M Cisilino), 162 (Bernard Dunne), 169 (David Morrison), 170 (Donald Fink), 183 top (Attila Jandi), 183 bottom (Prillfoto), 184 (Airi Pung), 185 (Ben Krut), 190 (Madrugadaverde), 191 top (Kevin George), 192 top (Cool Riff), 194/195 (Dovybaur), 200 (Miruna Nicoleswcu), 201, 202 (Michael Walsh), 203 (Mis. Maric), 204 top (Ciolca), 205 (Chon Kit Leong), 209 (Michael Harper), 211 (Arsty), 214 (Zastavkin), 215 (Veronikak), 216 bottom (Vander Wolf Images), 217 (Littleny), 219 top (Gary Stanex), 219 bottom & 220 bottom (Gazzag), 221 (Pajda83)

Fotolia: 29 (Kwiatek7), 189 (PCW)

Shutterstock: 6 (Magrugada Verde), 7 (Lukas Bischoff Photography), 8 (Neil Burton), 10/11 (Libor Kilmek), 12 & 13 (Maria Janus), 15 bottom (UTBP), 16 (J Rossphoto), 17 (Luca Fabbian), 18/19 (Peter Krocka), 21 (Patryk Kosmider), 22 (Logan Brown), 24 (Hugh O'Connor), 25 (MC2000), 26/27 (Alexilena), 28 top (EML), 33 (Paul J Martin), 34 & 35 (Patryk Kosmider), 36/37 (Pavel Voitukovic), 38, 39 (Shaun Turner), 40/41 (David Ortega Baglietto), 42 (Drakk Arts Photography), 44 (Louis-Michel Desert), 46/47 (Kevin George), 49 (Matthi), 50 (Stefano Valeri), 51 (Leo Pinheiro), 64 (Frederica Violin), 65 (Tom Whelton), 66/68 (Gigashots), 68 (Patryk Kosmider), 69 both (Kelleher Photography), 70 & 71 (Inalex), 72/73 (Drakk Arts Photography), 74 (Mikroman6), 76/77 (Gigashots), 78 (Patryk Kosmider), 79 (Morrison), 80/81 (D A J Holmes), 82 (Maria Janus), 85 (J Ross Photo), 90 (Arvydas Kniuksta), 91 top (Andrzej Bartyzel), 92 & 93 (Patryk Kosmider), 94/95 (Matthi), 97 (Patryk Kosmider), 100/101 (Shahid Khan), 104 (Green Pictures Media), 107 (Mike Drago), 108 (Drakk Arts Photography), 110/111 (Mark Carthy), 112 (David Soanes), 113 (D O'Brien), 114/115 (Gigashots), 116 (Maria Janus), 118 top (Evgeny Butusov), 118 bottom (Mark Carthy), 120 (Patrick Mangan), 122/123 (Mikroman6), 124 (Pavel Voitukovic), 125 (Frederica Violin), 126 (Kanuman), 127 top (UTBP), 127 bottom (Droneworx), 128 (Michal Ficel), 129 (EML), 130 top (Greg Fellman), 134 (Gabriel12), 135 (Ledokolua), 136 (Bartholemiej Rybacki), 137 (Alexilena), 138/139 (Ian Mitchinson), 144 (Alexilena), 147 (Julian Dewert), 154/155 (Lyd Photography), 156 (Patryk Kosmider), 158 (Inalex), 163 (Xavier Rouselle), 167 (Pecold), 176 bottom (Jean Renaud Photography), 177 (David O'Brien), 182 (Mikroman6), 186 (Richardzz), 193 (Stephen Long), 206 (Gabriel12), 207 (STLJB), 210 (Tyler W Stipp), 220 top (Richardzz)